I'm Not Really a Golfer

GW00983351

Jake Adie

jadie
BOOKS

Published by
Jadie Books Limited 2009

Copyright © Jake Adie 2009

ISBN 978 0 9561356 6 7

Cover illustration by Ian West

Typesetting by Jake Adie

Printed & bound by
York Publishing Services Ltd
64 Hallfield Road
Layerthorpe
York
YO31 7ZQ

For those who still have
a fairway to go

Other Not Really Titles

I'm Not Really 18 (female edition)
I'm Not Really 18 (male edition)
I'm Not Really 30 (female edition)
I'm Not Really 30 (male edition)
I'm Not Really 40 (female edition)
I'm Not Really 40 (male edition)
I'm Not Really 50 (female edition)
I'm Not Really 50 (male edition)
I'm Not Really 60 (female edition)
I'm Not Really 60 (male edition)
I'm Not Really 70 (female edition)
I'm Not Really 70 (male edition)
I'm Not Really Pregnant
I'm Not Really Getting Married (female edition)
I'm Not Really Getting Married (male edition)
I'm Not Really Moving House
I'm Not Really Retiring
I'm Not Really a Grandmother
I'm Not Really a Grandfather
It's Not Really Christmas
I've Not Really Passed My Test
I'm Not Really a Footballer
I'm Not Really a Rugby Player
I'm Not Really a Cricketer

Me, a Golfer?

Well, if owning a bag of assorted clubs, and queuing up to pay dues at the local municipal course each weekend means I'm a golfer then, okay, that's what I must be. But, comparing me to anyone even in the upper handicap zones who can reach the eighteenth hole without getting through a Saturday night lottery draw quota of balls, is simply making a nonsense of the sport. Okay, I have the necessary equipment, usually play at least one round each weekend and wear the requisite logo sweater, peaked cap and checked trousers. But that, I promise you, is where any similarity with real golfers ends and you'll have a hard job convincing me otherwise. Trouble is, I'd do absolutely anything to reverse this frustrating situation. Just to be able to turn up at the first green feeling even half equal to the other golfers around me would be comforting. Not that I've a problem keeping up with them score-wise. I mean, I've been known to go round in, now let me think, yes, I'm sure I've hit a ninety-eight sometime or other. Might have been a few years ago but I know I've done it. And it's not that I don't have the right technique. Might not be up to Tiger's standards but, well, if I concentrate hard enough, not many of the amateur players I spend my weekends with would collapse in fits of laughter at the sight of me teeing off. Well, actually, some *have* been known to but only when I've been having an off day. No, it's nothing like that. In fact, most of the time my non-golfer status would, I'm quite sure, go entirely unnoticed. It's more a case of the way I feel when I'm out there trying to look the part. Trying to look as though my whole performance, my whole approach to the game, my easy manner, is something that, sort of, comes naturally. Just like all the other enthusiasts around me. And it really doesn't matter what age or race they are or whether their handicap is in single or double figures, they just seem to exude a kind of oneness with most, if not all, aspects of their game. Just appear to be at ease with the sport in general. And I know what I'm talking about here because I've played rounds with most of them over the years. God, you'd think some of their naturalness would have rubbed off on me by now, wouldn't you. I mean, without even trying, it wouldn't be unreasonable to expect me to have, subliminally even, taken on board the way their game just seems to fall into place for them week after week. Like riding a bike for them, I suppose. For me, though, it's as though I fall off every time I get on the damn thing. Okay, everyone has good days and bad days, we all know that. But what I'm talking about is something much deeper. Let me explain: you see, when they drive a ball down the fairway they look as though they've got a pretty accurate idea of where it's going to land, give or take the odd twenty yards or so. But when I square up to the ball, I honestly haven't got the foggiest where it's heading. All right, nine times out of ten I pull off a reasonably decent shot but if anybody else on the course knew what was going on inside my head they'd wonder why I didn't take up something less taxing. Like noughts and crosses, maybe. And I'm absolutely sure they're aware of my non-golfing status but are just far too polite to let on. Look, don't laugh, but I'm really not completely sure when it comes to selecting an appropriate . . .

Well, come on, there're just too many to choose from, aren't there? Okay, I'm not going to start putting with a two wood, I'm not that silly. But that said, I've honestly never tried it. You never know. I'm sure Tiger Woods could sink a thirty-footer with a tennis racquet if he wished. But, then, I'm not Tiger Woods. No,

Club

my trouble is that I don't seem to be able to make an instant decision regarding which club to pull out of the bag relative to the nature of the shot. I'm sure I don't get it too wrong but, from the way I see it, everybody else turns to the bag and calmly selects the optimum club without appearing to give a second thought to whether it's going to do the job. As if they possess some kind of golf-friendly instinct. A sixth sense dedicated to all things golf. So, wanting to appear equally as cool and professional as these instinctive little upstarts, I feign to do precisely the same. But then, once I've made my choice and offered the club head up to the ball I think, "Jesus, what do you think you're doing?" And then I'm in no doubt whatsoever that everyone around me is sniggering behind their hands thinking exactly the same. And, believe me, trying to pull off a masterstroke when you're in that frame of mind is just not conducive to enhancing one's reputation. Quite intimidating, actually. So, what happens? I fluff the bloody thing. And vow, in future, I'll only ever go round on my own. Well it is all rather confusing, don't you think? I mean, as long as we have regulations limiting us to carrying a maximum of 14 clubs, I'm forever going to be stuck with having to make some sort of impossible shape/angle/weight-distribution/shaft-length decision no less than 14 times. And I don't find that easy. Look, consider, for a minute, the simple matter of the irons. Some few months ago, a pal of mine insisted that I should ditch my old four iron and equip myself with a cavity-back version. Sounded complicated to me. What difference was it going to make? I told him I had better things to do with my money than to waste it on some pseudo-scientific idea for extracting mega-millions from the golfing fraternity. I mean, did Arnold use a cavity-back? I doubt it. But my mate was adamant. Compared to what I'd been using he reckoned these ace pieces of kit were easily worth anything between five and ten strokes in even the most amateur of players' hands. "Ok, prove it." was my response. So we set up a 'scientifically-controlled' experiment all of our own which involved me placing a ball at the bottom of a steep incline immediately adjacent to the edge of the third green. A situation in which I'd probably go for my pitching wedge. So, with two identically angled tens with as near as matching grips, a carefully marked spot to where the ball was to be continually returned after each shot and even left and right foot position indicators, the experiment was ready to commence. I was handed one of the irons, not knowing which, and proceeded to make my first stroke — which shot a good two metres into the air before landing half-a-metre behind me. I was mentally willing it to have been the cavity-back. A second wedge was duly placed into my hands and, suspecting it was mine, I duly gave it my best shot. It dropped within inches of the hole. A large grin began to form on my face. We're not finished yet, I was told. Another club and another shot – this one having those behind me literally running for cover. A fourth club, another near hole. A fifth, into the rough. Sixth, plop, bull's-eye, straight down hole no. 3. "Okay, experiment over." said my adversary. "Every standard ten, totally out of control, every cavity-back, directly onto the green. With the final one right down the plughole!" I'd clearly lost the argument. "But hold on, give me my own wedge back and let me see how I fare without swapping with the cavity." I repeated the six-stroke exercise in precisely the same fashion and, surprise, surprise, achieved identical results. I offered what I felt was an appropriate, non-verbal gesture to my mate. Well, my performance was so bloody erratic it didn't matter what iron I used. Here, go fetch Tiger's tennis racquet, I thought. But it isn't all bad, actually. I do, after all, hold two golfing records. Honest. And the first one was a direct result of my electing to seek out some . . .

Pro Lessons

Thought it might be a good idea after our little 'controlled' experiment debacle. Although I suspected I was probably beyond help. He was a good guy, though. Friendly, obviously highly knowledgeable and, God, did his little private range have some equipment? If I was going to improve anywhere it'd be here, for sure. We started off by casually talking through my game, my perspectives on the various aspects. Watched a couple of DVDs. Drank some coffee. Then he asked me which particular technique I felt was primarily deserving of attention. How, on Earth, could I focus on just one? Okay, why not start at the beginning?, I thought. "Well, I'd rather go though my 'teeing-off' procedure if you don't mind." (Seemed, sort of, logical.) He planted me on a specially-designed mat with all sorts of optical equipment on one side and an enormous video screen on the other.

Presumably, he was going to carry out some kind of computerised, video analysis of me teeing off. Good God! "Right, before I intervene, just show me how you deal with this stroke. Ignore the apparatus around you. Take your time. Imagine it's any normal Saturday morning at the club." He was kidding, I'd probably take his head off! *Right, here we go. Just do your best. No point in trying to impress the guy 'cause he's seen it all before.* I carefully showed the business side of the high-tech wood he'd handed me, lined body and club parallel to target, feet well apart, ball well forward, club drawn back over right shoulder. . . "Stop, stop. My apologies. There's a gremlin somewhere in the equipment, an irritating 'thunk' noise when you shape up for your follow through. Okay, that should fix it. Try again." I took an extra deep breath, swung the shaft back. . . "Hold on, hold on, sorry, it's still there. Worse if anything." *Was he trying to unnerve me for some strange reason?* "Right, that should do it. Give it another go." Well, you wouldn't believe it but this went on for another fifteen minutes. And I was footing the bill, for God's sake. "Look, I'm so, so sorry but it just won't go away. Surely you can hear it." Well, I could, sort of, but it didn't sound like it was anything to worry about. Sort of noise you might hear anytime, I thought. Really didn't sound like a problem. Was this the guy's way of stretching out a lesson to earn a bit more dosh? Surely not. He was supposed to be a professional. "One more time. When you're ready." Then, all of a sudden, there was an almighty CRACK! The same sound but this time three times the volume. And it coincided precisely with me collapsing into a heap under the video screen with the most agonising pain in my left knee. His equipment was fine, save for some minor adjustments to the screen supports, but my knee was in need of some serious repair work. And there began my first golfing record. With the following three months spent under close, private healthcare scrutiny — on crutches and off work — I ran up a bill as long as the eighteenth fairway, drew zero salary and seriously considered applying for an entry in the Guinness's famous annual tome for having run up a bill for the most expensive golfing lesson on record. Not a good start. But my knee had benefited from a full MOT and I'd all but convinced myself that it had been the source of my problem all along. Plus, although unbeknown to me at the time, I was about to notch up a second golfing record on my very next attempt at . . .

Teeing Off

It was my first round after my three-month recovery and I was determined to prove to myself that the interruption was not going to make an ounce of difference to my progress. It was a busy morning at the club. Too busy, actually. But then, where else would any sane person rather be spending his time on such a perfect spring morning? With a sky that had, seemingly, been formed out of an unblemished, seamless sheet of stunning, azure fabric, I was about to begin what I felt certain would be an idyllic return to the golf course. Without a care in the world, I casually wandered, with golf bag in tow, from clubhouse to first tee in search of a likely-looking, unpartnered individual and soon chanced upon a guy of roughly my age looking to be every bit the ideal contender. And with me being the sort of company he'd no doubt enjoy immensely by giving a thoroughly good thrashing. But hey, this was my first game for months, the weather was a joy, the scenery right out of a picture book and my knee joint the pinnacle of anatomical excellence. By the time we arrived at the tee there were just two parties of three in front of us and one of four behind. Could have been worse. Just had to get my mind into gear. You know, rid myself of all those previous ideas of inadequacy. Well, we all get them, don't we? Anyway, I had a good excuse: I hadn't hit a ball for ages. A fact I took great care in bringing to the notice of my new friend in a voice carefully designed, also, to reach the ears of those queuing behind us. The two forward parties soon moved on without a great deal of fuss leaving me to square up and prove what I was made of. The nerves duly kicked in but I was determined not to allow them to get the better of me. I positioned the tee with a slight backwards slant for a little extra lift, as a mate of mine had suggested to me, pulled out my trusty driver, adopted what I felt was the perfect stance and whacked the ball for all I was worth. And, God, did it go? Way, way, way up. Way, way, way on. And way, way, way into the frigging copse a hundred yards, or so, to the right of the fairway. Jesus, this had to be the straightest, widest, rough-free fairway known to man. And I'd found the one, single group of trees for miles. Well, furlongs at least. My new acquaintance drove around the same distance but in a dead straight line landing his ball within yards of the copse. We strolled off together with me feigning an air of nonchalance hoping to give the impression that locating and hitting the ball onto the green was a mere formality. As if the angle from the copse might even offer an advantage. Think positively, I told myself. A couple of minutes later we arrived at the obstacle which we found, on closer inspection, to be even less of a hazard than it had at first appeared: three single quite immature beeches set in an insignificant patch of longish grass without a bush, a nettle, an adjacent stream or a ditch in sight. And all around, nothing but newly-mown turf for as far as the eye could see. Well, virtually. I mean, you'd have trouble losing one of your contact lenses in this spot let alone a golf ball. So, "My stroke first", I announced before confidently strolling over to where I imagined the ball was resting. It wasn't there. It wasn't anywhere. Well, the obstacle was so miniscule you could scan the whole bloody lot without turning your head. No rabbit holes, no worn away roots, no nothing. No golf ball. My mate wandered over to lend a hand. It still wasn't there. There could be only one explanation: it was lodged somewhere high up in one of the beeches. But these were young trees, barely more than saplings with less than half-a-dozen boughs between them. Honestly, almost every square inch of every branch was visible from where we were standing. But I was determined not to drop the shot. Couldn't bring myself to incur a penalty on my first stroke.

"Apologies, old chap but would you mind giving me a leg up?", I enquired. Although with the size of these trees an elbow-up might have been more appropriate. I carefully heaved myself, inch-by-inch, up the trunk doubting that it would carry my weight for any sustained period. The ball still wasn't there. The ball still wasn't anywhere. But we'd both seen it clearly enter the copse minutes before. It simply couldn't be anywhere else. Then, I spotted it. Well, not the ball, but a small, roughly-formed birds nest perched precariously in the apex of two slender boughs about three foot above me. Was I pushing my luck to climb further or should I just pay the price and get on with my 'third' stroke? No, I'd come this far and wasn't up for quitting. I went for it. And there it was, nestled, cuckoo-fashion, between three one-week-old, chirping balls of fluff. I immediately dispelled all thoughts of saving the shot and duly made my descent in the knowledge that I was very likely the first golfer ever to score three birdies with just one shot. And without a green in sight. But would I ever want to admit to it? However, not being one to give up easily, me and my highly-amused partner pressed on until a very strange incident occurred several holes later involving a group of . . .

And believe me, I might not be God's gift to the sport but I've never had any trouble getting on with those around me on the course. In fact, I've always found fellow golfers to be particularly amiable. You know, a good bunch of people to be around. Well, it's not surprising, is it. I mean, you're all gathered in the

Fellow Golfers

midst of some glorious countryside with acres of space between you and a good few miles away from your place of work. Couldn't be better. Why would anyone want to be anything but agreeable in such idyllic circumstances? And, of course, when it comes down to it, most folk, whatever their walk of life, are pretty decent. Invariably pleased to lend a helping hand if you're down on your luck. Pleased to offer a lift if the buses aren't running. Pleased to just, well, just, sort of get, along with you. Well, that's how I've always seen it and nowhere is it more evident than on the golf course. Until that first day back. Right, this is what happened, listen: there I was, or, rather, there we were, because by that time me and my new golfing pal were getting on like a house on fire. The embarrassment of my triple birdie incident, I suppose, did well to break the ice and in no time we'd developed a rapport. And then, all of a sudden, we heard the most awful commotion coming from some way behind us. Presumably on the previous hole. And we were totally oblivious to whatever, or whoever, it was due to the thick growth dividing the two fairways. We could certainly hear something but visually all was a perfect picture of peace and serenity. But then, some fifty or sixty yards away, a guy came rushing, into view as if there was no tomorrow. Truly panic-stricken by the look of it. Running for all he was worth. We immediately dashed over to a point about ten or fifteen yards to the right to get a view of the source of the racket only to witness what appeared to be a man and a woman standing over a guy lying stretched out on the ground with blood all over him. A mugging on the golf course? It just didn't make sense. But, believe me, things were not looking good for this poor fellow. The stationary man then began to give chase to the first guy and started shouting at the top of his voice, "Get the bugger, get the bugger". God, this is not what one expects to encounter on a sunny, spring afternoon on the golf course. But how could we ignore it? It came again, "Did you hear me, I said 'get the bugger, get the bugger'." He really meant it. I thought on my feet. And without further deliberation, did what could only be the decent thing: I made a dash for him. A dash for the 'bugger', that was. Well, I was an awful lot closer to him that his pursuer and, though I wasn't terribly keen on getting involved, I just couldn't bring myself to allow him to escape. I mean, the so 'n' so was clearly up to no good and there was I in a position to, possibly, bring the scoundrel to justice. And with my new reconditioned knee, I reckoned I had a distinct advantage over most individuals. I was off and, in under a minute, had got to within five yards of his heels. He was clearly flagging. I went for it. I leapt with all my might and, even though I say it myself, executed the most impressive rugby tackle you're ever likely to see this side of the Equator, catching him fairly and squarely around the thighs and delivering him face down smack onto the edge of a bunker. I got up. He didn't. He'd knocked himself clean out on a clump of hard earth surrounding the pit. But I wasn't worried, he'd come round in a minute or two. I was too busy feeling chuffed with myself. Had done my bit for the day, I thought. Who knows, might even get a slot on the local evening news. 'KNEE-OP GOLFER TRIES RUGGER ON MUGGER.' But then, right out of the blue, the pursuer appeared and, would you believe it?, he seemed to have it in for *me*. Good and proper, I can tell you. "What in Heaven's name do you think you're doing you idiot?" *You idiot?* What was this I was hearing? I'd just risked my own life chasing a villain, caught him, floored him and now had him sleeping like a baby waiting for the flashing blue lights to appear. "I just got the bugger", I proffered. "Isn't that precisely what you wanted me to do? You were yelling for all you were worth for someone to get the bugger, for God's sake." But it was another ground opening up moment for me. "I was shouting for him to get the buggy, you idiot. My mate's been whacked round the head with a number three iron, is losing blood at a rate of knots and with the help of a golf buggy we might just stand a chance of getting him off the course and into a hospital. Gulp! I did the decent thing. I ran for the buggy. You see what I mean? Not only do I have trouble getting to grips with the mechanics of the game, I'm no bloody good at anything when I'm anywhere near a golf course. Mm, maybe I'll stick to . . .

No, only joking. I mean, am I alone on this one? Isn't there anybody else out there who finds the idea of specially-designed facilities dedicated to the business of hitting a golf ball just a tad strange? Well think about it. I mean, can you name any other sport that deems it necessary to set up separate

Driving Ranges

establishments for the sole purpose of hitting their chosen design of ball? No, neither can I. And that's because there aren't any. So, why is that, ehm? Why do they go to all the trouble and expense to set up ball-bashing sites independent of the places they designate for actually playing the game? Well, that's easy to answer: people who play golf have got more money than they know what to do with. Simple as that. Other sportspersons of more modest means have to be content with practising their sports on the pitch/course/court/pool or wherever. Not that they wouldn't welcome the opportunity to enjoy the benefits of a dedicated rehearsal facility. Of course they would. But they don't have the spare dosh. Golfers are simply loaded. When a golfer is out driving around the countryside he's likely to chance upon a super, all-singing, all-dancing driving range, on average, once every twenty minutes. And it matters not a jot to him that he has to part with a few readies for the pleasure of smacking a bucketful of balls around the place for half-an-hour because he's minted. They all are. Okay, let's look at this from another perspective for a moment. Imagine the golfing fraternity were, in economic terms, no different to the rest of us. I know it's not easy but try to focus on the scenario best you can. Right, now picture, also, the complete absence of driving ranges. Like they've never been invented, yeah? Now, you're sitting at your bank manager's desk having just outlined your brilliant plan to open up a string of golf courses each of which will be totally devoid of fairways, bunkers, rough ground, greens, holes with flags sticking out, clubhouses, buggies, lakes, streams, countryside, competitions, social evenings etc etc. Instead, your wonderful new inventions will simply feature teeing off positions. On rubber matting. And once the ball was hit, nothing. And it mattered not whether the ball was hit well, badly or not at all. And you had to pay for the privilege. Right, who wants to guess what the bank manager's response might have been? Mm? Don't all shout at once. Exactly, he's doubled up on the Wilton broadloom in an uncontrollable giggling fit. Am I right? Of course I am. Now, if we fine tune a couple of the parameters to allow us to inform said banker that the enterprise will be strategically marketed towards only the most stinking rich members of society who, otherwise, have but not a clue what to do with themselves at weekends, how would you expect this to impact on his response? Need I say more? And there's another thing, the. . .

Silly expression. It's not a hole, it's a clubhouse. With a bar. And a bar held in incomparably high regard by golfers the world over. God, one could be excused for wondering why they don't arrange their courses with 18 bars and one hole. But, of course, even non-golfing golfers like yours truly appreciate a chance to take

Nineteenth Hole

things easy with a bevvie or three in the company of an assortment of like-minded individuals. Does, sort of, round off the day nicely, don't you think? A chance to take the previous couple of hours a little less seriously. To take ourselves less seriously. Yes, maybe 18 club bars wouldn't be too bad an idea. But, of course, there

is another side
to the clubhouse
that suggests
everything but
the adoption of a
lighter
perspective.
Certainly not all
about getting
things into
balance where
one can
experience a
bonding, a
oneness with
one's fellow
golfing folk.
Quite the
reverse, in fact.
You've only to
glance around

the walls to see the true essence of the establishment. Take a look next time you're enjoying your post match tipple. You'll find you'll be surrounded by permanent reminders of your humble abilities. Your constant failure to measure up to the status quo. Your utter uselessness. Because there before you on pristinely-preserved, mahogany plaques is a never-ending list of the names of golfers, in immaculate gilt lettering, who are better at it than you. Well, why do they do that? Why do they go to all that trouble and expense just to intimidate the vast majority of club members? Fee paying

members.
Members
without whose
hard-earned
cash the club
wouldn't exist.
Amazing or
what? Why
intimidate
everybody for
the glory of the
few? Not that the
glory is
particularly
warranted.
Take, for
example, the
'Hole-in-One'
commemorative
board. A
complete

disgrace, if you ask me. I mean, come on, give any top golfer of your choice a tee off at any hole of your choice and ask him to hole in one. I don't care who you pick: Tiger, Padraig, Jack, God, I don't care, Arnold, if you like. I'm easy about this. And give them ten goes at it. All right, 20. You choose. Because it'll make no difference. And that's because holes-in-one are pure luck. Nothing else, just complete and utter chance. If the finest exponents in the game can't do them when they try their hardest neither can anyone else. Is the club seriously suggesting that Fred Jones, chartered accountant from down the road, is superior to these legends? Well it would seem so, wouldn't it? Because, if he's not, they're simply celebrating luck. Not skill. Not aptitude. Not talent. Just L-U-C-K, luck. Jesus, they might just as well display the names of local lottery winners. Put their names up in big gold letters outside the town hall.

Yeah? So, after all's said and done, there aren't many aspects of the golfing world that I appear to be very much in tune with. Which adds up conclusively, I think, to my not really qualifying as a proper golfer. Agree? Mm, thought you would.